YOU DON'T KNOW WHAT YOU DON'T KNOW

CLEVELAND STATE UNIVERSITY POETRY CENTER
NEW POETRY
Michael Dumanis, Series Editor

John Bradley, *You Don't Know What You Don't Know*
Lily Brown, *Rust or Go Missing*
Elyse Fenton, *Clamor*
Dora Malech, *Say So*
Shane McCrae, *Mule*
Helena Mesa, *Horse Dance Underwater*
Philip Metres, *To See the Earth*
Mathias Svalina, *Destruction Myth*
Allison Titus, *Sum of Every Lost Ship*
Liz Waldner, *Trust*
Allison Benis White, *Self-Portrait with Crayon*

For a complete listing of titles please visit
www.csuohio.edu/poetrycenter

YOU DON'T KNOW
WHAT YOU
DON'T KNOW

John Bradley

Winner of the 2009 Cleveland State University
Poetry Center Open Competition

CSU Poetry Series
Cleveland State University Poetry Center
Cleveland, Ohio

First edition   5   4   3   2   1

This book is the winner of the 2009 Cleveland State University
Poetry Center Open Competition, selected by a jury comprised of
Kazim Ali, Mary Biddinger, Michael Dumanis, and Sarah Gridley,
and is a title in the CSU Poetry Series published by the Cleveland
State University Poetry Center, 2121 Euclid Avenue, Cleveland,
Ohio 44115-2214. www.csuohio.edu/poetrycenter, distributed by
SPD /Small Press Distribution, Inc. www.spdbooks.org

Cover image: Katherine Ace, "In the Beginning," Copyright 2010, used with permission.
You Don't Know What You Don't Know was designed and typeset by Amy Freels in Stone
Print with Bauer Bodoni display.

LIBRARY OF CONGRESS CATALOGING-IN-PUBLICATION DATA
Bradley, John, 1950–
You don't know what you don't know : poems / John Bradley. — 1st ed.
    p. cm. — (CSU poetry series)
ISBN 978-1-880834-90-9 (alk. paper)
I. Title. II. Series.

PS3602.R3427Y68 2010
811'.6—DC22   2009054200

Acknowledgments

Poems from this book have previously appeared in *ACM, Arsenic Lobster, Big Toe Review, Caliban, Diagram, Facets, Fine Madness, Floating Holiday, Jabberwock Review, The Kerf, Key Satch(el), Last Tangos, Luna, Out of Line, The Oval, Paragraph, Pemmican, Poetry Motel, The Prose Poem: An International Journal, Quick Fiction, Redactions, Sentence, Spout, Terminus, Terra Incognita*, and *VerbSap*.

Some of these poems have also been anthologized in *Add Musk Here*, Pavement Saw Press; *An Introduction to the Prose Poem*, Firewheel Editions; *The Best of the Prose Poem*, White Pine Press; *No Boundaries: Prose Poems by Twenty-Four American Poets*, Tupelo Press; *Online Writing: The Best of the First Ten Years*, Snowvigate Press; *The Rose Metal Press Field Guide to Prose Poetry*, Rose Metal Press; *(Some from) Diagram: A Print Anthology*, Del Sol Press; and *States of Common Rapture*, Red Pagoda Press.

With love and gratitude to Ric and Bonnie Amesquita, Bob Edwards, Ed Dougherty, Jean and Joe Gastiger, Ray Gonzalez, Jim Grabill, Kent Johnson, Peter Johnson, George Kalamaras, Ken Letko, Becky Parfitt, Susan Porterfield, Bill Witherup, Phil Woods, Dieter Zeschke, and most of all, Jana.

for Joe Gastiger, my favorite prose poet

Contents

Whence It All Began   3

I Think I Hear Radioactive Angels Singing Doowop in the Crabapple Tree

Parable of Wood and Hole   7
Parable of the White House Replica   8
Noah's Ark Found on Mars   9
Jared Fogle Lost 245 Lbs.   10
Parable Embedded with Patience and Impatience   11
Parable of the Astral Wheel   12
Parable of the Pony Syndrome   13

I Think I Hear Epistolary Wind Blab in the Respiratory Chimney

I Shall Be Released   17
Parable of the Permeable Wardrobe   18
Parable of the Twisted Tangle   20
Ask Anyone   21
Chimney Sleep   22
Re: The Parameters of Professorial Sleep   23
I Never Button the Top Button of My Shirt Because It Makes My Head
    Look Too Big   24
Memo to Ariadne   26

I Think I Hear Lightning in the Brain Chasing an Insoluble Sigh

This Flammable Earth   29

Parable in Which Gillian Shrieks   30

Carnival, Paris (woman reading behind stage)   31

My Father's "Yealh"   33

Why J. Robert Oppenheimer Translated Allen Ginsberg's *Howl*
   into Sanskrit   34

Rain Dispatch   36

Yawn   37

I Think I Hear the Repertory Ensemble Frogs in a Place of Pause

History, Indigestion, and Love   41

Footnote to Xu Bing's *Dust*   42

The Infinity of the Finite, Or Why My Name Comes Up Whenever
   a Sinkhole Is Found   43

Leni Riefenstahl, The Final Installment   45

In the Shop of Tin Noses   47

Edward Teller, Father of Further and Farther   48

Footnote to a Line by Fernando Pessoa   50

(Let Us All Reflect a Moment Upon) Dick's Hatband   52

I Think I Hear the President Commuting the Silence of a Meandering Carnivorous Sentence

Number Theory   57
Parable of the Indeterminable Cave   58
I Was John and Cindy McCain's Indentured Servant   59
Parable of the Unclean Litter   60
Sam Cooke Teaches Richard Nixon the Twist   61
Confessions of a Ladder Rider   62
Sometimes My Skin Flies Off in Tiny Particles and Then Some Time
    Later Flies Back and Acts As If It Never Left, But That Has Nothing
    To Do with What I'm About to Tell You   63
All the Ape-Gone Songs   64

I Think I Hear the Last Transmission in a World of Lastlessness

The Figure in the Flux   67
Parable of the Hair Chair   68
You Too Can Apologize to the Moon   69
Don't Blame the Chalk; I'd Rather Be Servicing Mr. & Mrs. Caulk   70
Asleep Inside a Bird   72
Sustain   74
Crown   75

You don't know what you don't know.

JOHN NEGROPONTE

YOU DON'T KNOW WHAT YOU DON'T KNOW

Whence It All Began

Once, when there was only one word for people, and it was the same word as for the earth, I was human, with a body for a body, skin for skin, teeth for teeth, and hair. Hair everywhere. After I left a place where I had slept, hair grew from the soil. But I was not afraid of Hair, just of the things Hair wanted me to do. Hair told me to climb to the top of a hollow tree and jump. Hair told me that I would fly—all the vibrating little hairs vibrating, carrying me on the wind. Hair told me to make love with my cousin the poplar. I knew this was wrong, to make the trees have children. They would walk the land day and night on two legs saying, "Am I a tree? Am I a human? Am I a human tree?"

So I tore out my hair. I tore it out in handfuls. I threw it on the ground. I sprinkled salt on it. Hair growled. Hair wept. Hair promised never to flagellate Hair with my hair. I stood there, looking at Hair dying in the grass. I knew Hair spoke lies. Hair would never change because Hair was Hair. I ran away. Hair found me again. But only some of Hair could tolerate me. The rest burned when it tried to root in me, leaving upon my skin scars the shape of crescent moons. Now I am naked, nearly naked, Hair hiding in my armpit and groin and crotch. And they ask me, those last survivors of Hair, what I cannot ever know—"Are you hair? Are you human? Are you human hair?"

I Think I Hear Radioactive Angels Singing Doowop in

the Crabapple Tree

Parable of Wood and Hole

I was born in a watery hole in the woods, although my mother claims it was an island of woods surrounded by water. My father is napping in front of the Vikings game right now, so he's unavailable for consultation. Not that he'd recall. The knee would be a terrible place to give birth from, what with the hard shell and the constant bending and occasional kneeling.

Just yesterday I knelt when trying to expel a lumpy bump of air caught in my throat, another bad place to birth from. A baby born from the knee would constantly cry to go outside and worm its way up a tree, and then cry to be lowered down, and then cry to be hoisted up for the wind to tease. Some sharks prefer tea and honey to blood, and some give birth to feathers.

After a few hours, the knee aches and shakes, and pretty soon little blue-gray bugs start coming out and there's a war going on in a country where homes resemble garages. Some of these garage-homes hide weapons made from broken electric can openers and discarded typewriters. The enemy knows that to break the back you attack the knee, thus the waterous holes in the trees.

Parable of the White House Replica

I can still remember the day a cloud of ammonia covered the White House and I was called in to pull the President out of the bathtub. I eat a boiled egg and an unboiled egg each day to heighten my balance. It must be difficult to have to walk through the White House naked, even if they let you keep on your socks and shoes. I couldn't find anyone in the presidential bathtub, nothing except the mannequin leg once worn by Martha Washington.

It was a good thing they had a spare copy of the President down in the basement. All they had to do was send a few volts through him and he was waving his hand and signing his name to everything within reach. Sometimes I add a dash of powdered reindeer antlers to my eggs. Then I start singing "Don't Fence Me In." You can still see some of the presidential signature, if you look carefully, behind my right ear. Sort of looks like it says *Killallamoeba*.

Then the President's wife, or someone dressed like her, snuck in without paying to see the exhibit of the broccoli replica of the White House. It was no bigger than the harp used by Henry Kissinger when he played "Who Do You Love?" with Bo Diddley. Sometimes I eat just the boiled egg, but I make sure I eat a raw egg within the next forty-eight hours. I never wash behind my ears. I can't bear to erase our disappearing American history.

Noah's Ark Found on Mars

In the movie version, Noah, played by George Clooney, sells his soul to the Devil, played by George Steinbrenner, for the movie rights. Noah's log reads, *In the movie version, I hope they let me wear a loin cloth and recite* "The Road Not Taken." In the human waste recycling room, the teacher, Cher, played by George C. Scott, sings about the principal, played by Jorge Luis Borges, who won't let her teach class wearing only lingerie. Everyone is afraid of the Security Chief, the robot with the voice of George Patton, who can deal blackjack, provide open heart surgery, and perform oral sex all at the same time. Meanwhile the Mad Scientist, played by George Foreman, clones a race of pith-helmet-wearing dwarves, played by George Will. They chew tobacco and recite "The Road Not Taken" in a George Jones accent. When the oil pipeline is attacked by Crazy Horse, played by George Clinton, the preacher, played by George Orwell, smuggles rocket propelled grenade launchers hidden inside Bibles to the Amazon Queen, played by Phyllis George. Noah's wife, played by Georgia O'Keeffe, runs off with Crazy Horse and they form KrazyWorks, an interstellar corporation that controls water rights and sex education. Robert Johnson, played by George Hamilton, falls in love with Crazy Horse's daughter, played by George Stephanopoulos, who teaches Johnson how to play the blues. In the final scene, God, played by George Steinbrenner, clutches his crotch just before Crazy Horse, now played by George Thorogood, played by George Tenet, launches a nuclear strike. "Very little disturbs me," God muses, still clutching his crotch, "which means very little pleases me, which means very little disturbs me." As the camera slowly retreats into the stars, the Surgeon General, played by Boy George, backed by a techno-Afro-Afghan band, sings from the Red Planet, "I took the Ark less traveled by, and that has made all the difference."

Jared Fogle Lost 245 Lbs.

There he was on national TV, Jared Fogle, claiming it was him, not the shed poundage, who was the real Jared Fogle. "Whenever I smell mendacity, I get hungry." Those were the shed poundage's first words. Last seen wearing one black shoe and one brown shoe, the shed poundage was thought to be armed, slightly dangerous. You can ask Zena, who used to be Serena, until I bought her the Vegas showgirl costume. She took the job at the Indian casino and that was that. Because no one is immune from the phrase "to shed pounds while you sleep."

What did she leave me with? What did she leave me with? The empty gerbil cage, a jar of jalapeño mustard, Bipolar Barbie, male and female genitalia. Back when she was Serena, we used to make love on the roof, though the roof may say I was a part-time custodian who believed every day was Sunday, the one day we could make love, because rapture, said Serena, creates an electrical charge that builds up in the joints and causes premature arthritis. "What's Swiss cheese without the holes," says Zena, who is technically no longer my girlfriend but technically bound to both Jareds and me through the shared blood transfusion.

As soon as I saw him on the TV commercial stretching out his trouser waist where he and the other Jared used to live, I called Zena and we talked about the time we ate at the Subway and she lost five pounds right before my eyes just from the rigorous machinations of her jaw on the whole wheat sub. "I'm okay with it," I said to Zena about Jared the Subway celebrity, because I am ok with it, because what can a TV commercial like that do for you, really, but leave you with a closet full of empty pants.

Parable Embedded with Patience and Impatience

One bomb was stuck in his lower stomach and another in his upper back. He didn't know how they got there, but as long as they didn't go off he didn't much care. The doctor who was a mechanic by day and a doctor in the evening said it would be too risky to try and remove them. "And expensive," his mother added. "Go on with your everyday chores," the doctor advised. "Just don't bump into any walls or slam yourself down into chairs. You should be fine."

On the way home, his mom bought him a dish of ice cream. He didn't even have to ask. As he ate, she looked down at the ice cream and sighed. "There could be a bomb in the ice cream," she said. "You never know. I have one lodged inside my wrist, but I've never told your father. It would only make him sad. Besides, he has one stuck in the back of his head. You mustn't say anything about this. I only tell you so you won't act as if you're special."

On the way out, he bumped into the door. Not very hard. Just hard enough to see if the bombs were angry. If they were angry, it wouldn't matter how careful he was. But with happy bombs, he could do anything. Maybe it was the ice cream that made them happy. Patience and Impatience, that's what he'd call them. He'd have to find a way to get money for ice cream for Patience and Impatience. Maybe he could sell more firewood or haul more water from the well. "You look so grown up today," said his mother, rubbing his head, "so handsome."

Parable of the Astral Wheel

"I wonder where your brother is," my father says, puffing on his briar pipe at the train station, gazing up at the portly pigeons in the rafters. The station has been closed for decades, but I don't tell him. "Should have been here hours ago," he notes. I ask if I can polish his shoes. I open the wooden barrel that serves as my stool and storage unit, find the ox blood polish, open the can and spit into the polish as he taught me to do when I was a child. He pretends to read *Time* magazine, but I know he's studying my every move. When I'm done buffing his shoes to an obnoxious shine, I sit back and wait. He glances down at his shoes and says, "Just a little more spit."

I ask him if he'd like a pack of gum, a comb, a condom, radioactive tumbleweed, an astral wheel. "I wonder," he says, "what's keeping your brother." I don't tell him that my brother is dead. "He never would have left, you know, if I had read the Bible every day," he tells me. "You'll like the astral wheel," I tell him. "It's completely silent and no one can see it, and your every movement spins out a prayer." He shakes his head. "If only we had listened to the priest," he says, "and when he was a baby had his little butt sewn shut."

Parable of the Pony Syndrome

"Pony," I say to my mother, and then stop, horrified. How could I call my own mother "Pony?" I can't apologize, as I don't want to draw attention to my faux pas.

"The sun is a byproduct of honey," I tell her, "and thus you and I will get sticky if we stay in the sun too long."

"Is something wrong, Pony?" she asks. "Tell your Pony."

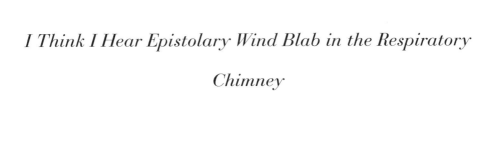

I Think I Hear Epistolary Wind Blab in the Respiratory Chimney

I Shall Be Released

I once dated a woman who had a miniscule role (she bit the head off a marigold) in a movie that was never released but gained cult status mostly because it was never released. "Doesn't faze me," she'd tell me, but I wondered why she used the word "released" for making love, as in, "Let's get released," instead of "Let's make Milwaukee moan," or "Let's boil the carpet," or "Let's cremate the goldfish."

Whenever I took a photo of her, she pulled a strand of hair over one eye, or shook her head so hair covered her face, or stood so that you could only see her staring back at you through one eye. "Is Renee feeling all right?" my mother asks me in the kitchen. "She seems a little, you know." "She's fine, really, mom," I tell her. "She's just waiting to be released."

Rolling down the driveway, thinking about the taste of marigolds, I command my right foot to stomp upon the brake, but my foot says, "Commander, that order is not a feasible option at this particular moment in perpetual time," so the unslowed car plows into the neighbor's organic kabuki garden. For this I must admit I gained a certain level of renown on that street and several interconnected streets adjacent thereto.

Parable of the Permeable Wardrobe

Along the curb in front of the house, a large wooden wardrobe waits to be carried away. I look inside for an overcoat or perhaps a life preserver. There's my mother, beside a small inflatable pool, painting her toenails, cotton balls between her toes. "Don't ever underestimate the power of a cotton ball," she advises me.

*

The telephone, in the shape of an eggplant, rings. It's a private historian for the Carnegie Foundation. He says my fingerprints were found on an axe handle used to kill one of Andrew Carnegie's Pinkerton agents at Homestead. "But I wasn't even alive then," I protest. "Ah, and if you were one of the strikers then, Mr. B.," he asks, "tell me, just what would you have done?"

*

"Say you were approached at a party by a cockroach in a tux," says a cockroach in a tux at the party. He totters on his hind legs, thus jostling the too-large eyeglasses on his head. "Would you inform the cockroach that he was merely a cockroach perched on hind legs, wearing glasses much too large for his head? Or would you join him in discussing the long range ramifications of storing plutonium in glass logs?"

*

"This is how monks in Japan prevent cancer," says my mother, sliding off her rings, pouring baby oil into one hand, rubbing both hands together, then working the oil into her tanned skin. "I try to warn your father, but he never hears a thing I say." She sighs, then takes a swig of her Johnson & Johnson Baby Oil.

*

Underneath my left armpit, the skin splits and I see part of a television screen embedded there. In the sole of my foot, another piece of screen. Behind my ear, another. "Am I turning into a television?" I ask at the clinic. "Hmmm?" says the doctor, watching the *Lassie* rerun on the TV screen under my armpit. "Just keep your arm raised, son."

Parable of the Twisted Tangle

"Well," she said, "I'll let you, just this once, shave my legs, but under one condition. You wear your white Teddy-Roosevelt-visiting-the-site-of-the-Panama-Canal suit, with white pith helmet, white spats, and black cane."

"Only if you wear your Jack-the-Ripper-street-slut dress, with torn hem and unwashed petticoat," I replied.

"Only if you do Norman Bates, in his mommy's long button down dress, lipstick smeared over your lips," she countered.

"Only if you do Generalissimo Franco disguised as Madame Curie disguised as Federico Garcia Lorca," I demanded.

"Only . . . ," she began. Meanwhile, the hair on her legs continued to tangle and twist.

Ask Anyone

An overturned-behind-the-garage wheelbarrow bearing sleep fell asleep in an overgrown backyard. And so I find it difficult to say to this day if the body is clay or flame. Maybe that's why I prick my finger each time I touch Mistress Raspberry or Lord Nipple. Fewer in the rain can know whether the skinless droplet ignites as it enters the skull. Hair of sleeping trees, hair of the man living in his gravel car, hair of red-headed boy smoked in leafy reefers. Growth in the armpits and groinal cavities making each of us finite rain forest. Ask the Vice President why he's spreading weed killer on his waffle.

Week after week in my defoliated chest I hear Dan Rather a week too soon or a week too late. Even after repeated beatings with umbrella and extension cord, the aroma of rain can be found in motel towel. JFK and RFK, each with pricked forefinger, napping inside the coat closet. Infinite frogs wandering our power lines to and fro. Waffles woven on roofs to protect all below from befalling woe. Even if it could be surgically removed, there's something heinous and famous about the driven anus. Ask the Vice President why the rodent population doesn't deserve a rise in the molecular wage.

Though little with molecular confidence can be stated, much is often stated confidently. Hair of wakeful waffle, hair of the woman watering her wig, hair of red-headed boy available now in time delay capsule form. Infinite frogs bumping to and fro in our blood platelet cities. A row of Marilyn Monroes, each more Marilyn than the last. Call me Rocco, or Bongo, or Boyo. In the outback behind the garage, the stillness keeps fully asleep, with something of me fueling the sleeping, and the sleeper vining round all around.

Chimney Sleep

Unable to get to sleep one hot summer night, I climb out of my window and onto the roof. Plumping my pillow against the base of the chimney, I notice something I've never seen before: a row of tiny houses, the ones I'd built for my miniature railroad trains years ago. Someone mortared them into place at the base of the chimney. I peek in the window of a tiny plastic brick house. A map with pastel ice floes on the wall over the bed, and, oh, the bed sheets—Dreamsicle cool. I run into the house, up the stairs, and dive for the bed, tingling with sleep before I land.

*

I'm delivering mail, decades old, stashed in the trunk of my English teacher's old Volvo. He claimed he had no idea how all that mail got there. I can still remember the day he took our class to the post office and told us, "Every letter written is a letter written to God." Maybe, if he's lucky, they'll let him teach English in prison. When I deliver the undelivered mail, men salute me, women embrace me, dogs urinate all over themselves.

*

Clatter of aluminum ladder leading up to the chimney. My father's voice, swearing at me for leaving his ladder out. Through the blinds I see the trunk of his enormous thumb, large and powerful in the moonlight. Much too large to ever enter my little brick house. How can I tell him. God is a postal worker dozing off in his postal uniform upon a mound of mail, letters lightly falling from the sky.

Re: The Parameters of Professorial Sleep

"I think Professor Sleepmask might be sleeping under his sleepmask while he's lecturing," suggests Anhedonia. "He lectured for three and a half hours last Wednesday, and he never noticed that one class left and another came in, and another left and another came in. And they weren't even his classes."

"Well, I like Professor Sleepmask's class," states Tantalus. "I nap during his lectures, and it never bothers Professor Sleepmask."

"Maybe Professor Sleepmask wears his sleepmask while he lectures," muses Euphoria, "so he can treat the goofball students the same as the kiss-ups."

"Have you ever taken a close look at Professor Sleepmask's sleepmask?" inquires Catatonia. "It's got these little pink skiers on it, each one wearing a Professor Sleepmask sleepmask."

"I sure don't want to be around when Professor Sleepmask takes off his sleepmask," shudders Panacea. "I mean, what if you can see his brains right through his eyes?"

"I don't know about that," replies Anhedonia, "but I think Professor Pajamas might be snoring inside her nightgown while she's lecturing."

I Never Button the Top Button of My Shirt Because It Makes My Head Look Too Big

My wife, his wife, our wife sits in bed with the lamp on, as we pretend to sleep, one husband on each side of her, and let her pretend to read.

I married her first, and then after the wedding, on the steps outside the church, he married her, and then, in the car driving us away from the church, I married her again, just to be sure.

She doesn't mind, she says, having two husbands, as long as we don't ever bother her with a request for sex. Of course not, we agree. So we have sexual encounters downstairs with the large, soft chair, each of us making love to the same chair arm at the same time.

When she takes her bath in the morning, and again later in the evening, we take turns. I scrub her back and shoulders, he scrubs her front and legs. She won't let either of us near her toes.

Sipping begonia tea in the morning, she sits in her stuffed chair, the one we have marital relations with at night, and reads the paper. I make a cup of coffee for me and her other husband. He makes toast for her. She says her toast is burnt and waves it away. Then I eat her toast.

"Do you want the left or right side?" he asks. "You can have the right side tonight," I tell him, as we take our positions with the chair. When we get divorced, I know what will happen. We will fight, me and him, in front our wife, over who gets the overly loved chair. And the chair will say, "Please, you think I want either of you?"

Memo to Ariadne

I'm going to need a change of address, a change of clothes, a motion that's a cross between a shamble, a dodge, and a faint. I'm going to need spelunker bread, avuncular bread, homuncular bread, dusted with arsenic. I'll need nude photographs of Cindy Crawford in the arms of James Dean in the arms of Walt Whitman. I'm going to need a recipe for lightning: how much insomnia, how much caffeine, how much flea powder. I know I'm going to need the phone number of someone with Salt somewhere in their last name. I'm going to need a way out, a way in, a way back, a way forward, a way to rest along the long way. I'm going to need a book with the caption *Morning's center is always noon* underneath a color photo of Crazy Horse entombed in a space suit. I'll need a used Buick with a radio that plays the soundtrack of that Jean Cocteau movie where he's listening to the car radio. I'll need a map of Dixon, Illinois, egg yolk stains at the bottom right. I'm going to need railroad brandy, hummingbird brandy, clairvoyant brandy. I know I'm going to need a spare prostate. I'll need a copy of the Zapruder film soaked in Visine. I'll need Amelia Earhart's aortal and dental records. I'll need a guarantee of amnesty, a plea for clemency, a pardon for unforeseen acts of malice and mercy. I'm going to need a song with the refrain *Noon's center is always morning*. I'll need amniotic samples, a disinterested party, a parry, an opening, a counterclockwise password, an alibi, an operator, a distressed identity, a passport, a Swiss bank account, bilingual inoculations, an antidote to the official antidote. I know I'm going to need a portapotty. Don't forget a pair of plague gloves. When you see me at the market beside the paprika stand, tap the side of your nose three times.

I Think I Hear Lightning in the Brain Chasing an

Insoluble Sigh

ר

This Flammable Earth

As the earth is flammable, a man takes to spitting to his left and right. "Why are you spitting so?" asks his wife. "I don't know yet." "You mean at some point you'll know why you're casting your slobber about?" "Well, I could run out of spittle first."

As the earth is flammable, a woman takes to spitting ahead and behind. "Why are you spitting so?" a man asks his wife. "What are you talking about? You're the one who's spritzing his spittle about." "You have no idea you're lactating at this very moment?" "Now milk is a form of spittle?"

As the earth is flammable, a man and woman take turns spitting. "To safeguard you from the flames," says the husband, spitting upon his wife. "To safeguard the flames from you," says the wife, spitting upon her husband.

As this text is flammable, a spitwad somewhere is taking form. "Spitwise, I'm growing tired from so much saliva," says a reader, who is not yet born, yet already flammable.

Parable in Which Gillian Shrieks

Tad stopped Leslie as she was about to suffocate David, and he brought Bart's dead body to the mental ward. This led to a battle between Asa and Ben, who suddenly figured out that Gina runs the mob family. At Wildwind, Gillian shrieked when she discovered Greenlee's diabetic cash. As Jack showed Greta his new house, he tripped and fell on top of her, forcing Jennifer and Hope to use the school shower. Kay plunged into the hellfire to save Miguel, who had gone after Charity, who realized she isn't Deacon. Ridge found Taylor chained to the fireplace grate, prompting Ethan and Theresa to almost make love. As Chad and Luis sought help from Father Lonigan, Sam tried to stop Ethan from being sucked into hell, and started to lose his grip as he was attacked by Cristian's fake ID business. Mimi and Jan launched their plot against Chloe in chemistry class, where an explosion sent chemicals into her hair, forcing Josh to realize he isn't in Bianca's journal. As Luke finally began to decode the disks, Roy took a bullet in the stomach while rescuing a captive Melissa from the junkie sealed in a crate by R.J. Helena showed the Ice Princess to Lucky, sparking a programmed response that prompted Liz to use the school shower. Todd wanted to flee with Blair to another country, but Rick had to choose between the federal authorities and a computer geek who doesn't want to have a baby. Jake let Taggert's liver transplant out of the bag, and Ridge drew a connection between Steffy's drawing and the pregnant dogs outside Morgan's house. Lucky seduced Austin, but Sami reacted badly to the revenge medication. Raul collapsed but Dixie's presence brought Lucky back to world trash consciousness. As Cookie waited for Frank in 1973, he and Karen ran into Rhonda at Kelly's in 2001. Coming: At Wildwind, Gillian shrieks over the unearthed baby geek's DNA sample.

Carnival, Paris (woman reading behind stage)

1926, GELATIN SILVER PRINT, ANDRÉ KERTÉSZ

Paris: where a photograph entinctures _____.

The folding chair: linger the body into thirds.

Her ballet slipper: twine around the eye.

Backstage light: a crushed, crushable kiss.

The man cut in half by art: feels no back strain.

Her sly right foot: slightly upward cocked.

Heavy lips: the smell of an armpit's damp.

Too puffy fur cuff: borrowed from a seance.

Her wedding ring: the science of silence.

A burdened book: read into this what you will.

Her high top hat: coughing the invisible man.

1926: when I _____ and sometimes _____.

Flower behind her ear: Hemingway for the masses.

Working class nose: book without body, body without book.

André Kertész: slow disappearance of luck.

My Father's "Yealh"

Was that an "l"? That's what I thought when I first heard my father say: "Yealh." That reassuring word "yeah" with a not-so-reassuring "l" cutting in near the end. Not at the very end, because there was a carry-over of the vowels bleeding out and around the "l." No, that can't be right, I thought. I must have misheard. So I listened, day after day, capturing and discarding the usual "yeahs," before it happened. My mother's call as he watched a New York Giants football game: "Jack." And then he let slip: "Yealh."

How exactly did that unlikely, unlikeable "l" get there? Maybe it started as a composite of: "Yeah, I will." But why haven't I ever heard anyone else utter this contraction? And besides, his tone wasn't right for "yeah, I will." It was more like: "You know, I hear you and don't hear you at the same time." Or: "What would you say if I told you that my leg was being swallowed by the cosmos?" Or: "You know, I can, am processing your words, but if you ask me later I won't remember a damn thing." Or sometimes: "I wonder what they're doing right now in hell." When no one was around, I'd practice in my bedroom: "Yealh," I'd say to the window. "Yealh," to the scruffy clouds. "Yealh," to the back of my bedroom door. Only my "yealh" was tinny, self-conscious. His: wispy, inscrutable.

I've never spoken of this to anyone, especially not my mother. She won't want him to be remembered as: The Man Who Invented "Yealh." I leave it to you, then, to ignore this neologism, or to pass it on, saying it when you're preoccupied, or not sure you want to agree, or on those occasions you feel the cosmos nibbling at your toes. Swirling down the discord ear, "Yealh," your quiet statement of qualified affirmation.

Why J. Robert Oppenheimer Translated Allen Ginsberg's *Howl* into Sanskrit

1. If he didn't, the Finns, the Poles, the Turks would.

2. Teller wanted to translate *Moby Dick* into haiku, dog biscuit, sunglasses, a cold beer, pineapple pizza, Marilyn Monroe in a silk kimono singing "Happy Deathday to You." When she kissed you, you'd explode into Moby Dick. It's not clear if Teller meant the book or the whale or some combination of both.

3. The F.B.I. taped him speaking to someone named "Three-Personed God" concerning Oppenheimer's vision of driving his car as far east as the car would run and then expiring there in the front seat beside J. Robert Oppenheimer: pipe, porkpie hat, piece of welder's glass.

4. The "J" in J. Robert Oppenheimer, he once stated in an interview, does not stand for Jew, jollification, japonica, Janus-faced Julius Caesar, Jerusalem thorn, jujube, *j'accuse,* jellyroll, joystick, jabberwocky, jackanapes, jujutsu, jury-rigged, Judas, Jell-O tremors, or Joint Committee to Defuture Fascist Salival Dreamings.

5. In her diary, Kitty Oppenheimer writes, "And when we make love, he yells: *I am Oppenheimer, scatterer of worlds.*"

6. Oppenheimer once came upon Teller in his office smoking a joint. He looked at Oppenheimer, and Oppenheimer looked at him. Teller held out the joint

as if to say, "Well?" Oppenheimer looked down, as if to say, "Why are you smoking leather shavings from your prosthetic foot?" Teller tilted his head to one side, as if to state, "Why not?" Oppenheimer backed out of Teller's office, as if to say, "One day you too will betray me."

7. If he didn't, the F.B.I., General Motors, Mickey and Goofy would.

8. The "J" stood for Nothing, he explained, which stands for Whoever Done Did You Gonna One Day Undone You, which stands for Each Time I Inhale On My Pipe I'm Burning Another Piece Of The Void, which stands for J. Edgar Hoover, Why Don't You Take a Good Long Look Up God's Ass?

9. As far as associating with RED: Oppenheimer claimed RED was depressed and suicidal at the time. Oppenheimer admitted spending a night with RED to comfort her, but it has never been proven that his face, hands, or teeth were actually stained from the contact.

10. When we make love, he yells: *I am Oppenheimer, shatterer of words.*

11. To cure his throat cancer, Oppenheimer shredded John Hersey's *Hiroshima* and gargled with it thrice daily.

12. Oppenheimer never finished his translation. Where Ginsberg urges America to "Go fuck yourself with your atom bomb," Oppenheimer notes in the margin: "Not physically possible at this particular time."

Rain Dispatch

It's raining: right now somebody somewhere is doing something stupid. It's raining: a flannel shirt hibernating in a plastic grocery bag slowly uncoils. It's raining: I'm only telling you this so I don't have to tell you something worse. It's raining: the walking woman in the black leather coat goes about her routine as if it's not raining. It's raining: first I think it's a list, then a curse, then a prayer one says when tasting fear. It's raining: on the mossy roof, the musky leaves, the unrepentant cigarette filters by the curb. It's raining: the moon's foggy fingers seep through every chamber. It's raining: I consider and reconsider the possible angles for making love with you in the pantry. It's raining: every droplet is cause and effect and at the same time neither cause nor effect. It's raining: into the scalding water in mom's spaghetti pot, dad pours some baking powder and soaks his foot. It's raining: he doesn't even have to say, "Don't tell your mother." It's raining: I can't remember if I already told you this. But whether I did or didn't, it's raining. A piece of newspaper under the back porch bleeds into black soil. It's raining: the ant reservoirs finally begin to fill. This morning I don't have to swallow anything except this. It's raining.

Yawn

It's Sunday morning on the sofa, and he can hear his name being called from the next room, but my father can't move. He's in a hardware store in Lynbrook, looking at row after row of screws. None of them seem to match the screw he has in his hand, which belongs to . . . he can't remember what. He can hear his name coming from behind him, or below, or above. He yawns. The yawn's so heavy, so cumbersome, he feels its weight pushing him down to the dusty wooden floor, where he curls and soon begins to snore.

Not all yawns are to be feared. Sometimes on a late December-early January afternoon my father yawns, and I see—inside the yawn—a green pear, just out of reach, ripening, perpetually ripening.

I Think I Hear the Repertory Ensemble Frogs in

a Place of Pause

History, Indigestion, and Love

Mussolini's chin rests on the dining room table. Like a cantaloupe rind scoured calmly and cleanly, with no drop of juice escaping, the chin attests to nothing but itself. How could this have happened?

"You know I didn't do it," says Pat Summerall. "When I'm not announcing football games, I'm in my socks and boxers taking a nap in the trailer."

"Well, I certainly didn't do it," says John Madden. " I love football, and my wife, and the flag, and my bus, and Buffalo wings, and all those people out there who love big guys like me."

"Don't look at me," says President Bush. "Maybe this Massolinguini fellow was a terrorist," he adds. "You never know where they transpire from."

"Then how did it get here? Where did it come from?" asks John Bradley, rubbing his side, where a long, curved scar recently appeared.

"And just who, if you don't mind my asking, are you?" muses Pat Summerall, waking from a brief nap.

"How does it get so dusty in here," sighs my mother, taking a feather duster to Mussolini's chin, scattering it into infinitesimal particles.

Footnote to Xu Bing's *Dust*

"As there is nothing from the first
Where does the dust collect itself?"[1]

---

1. Note the pocked yellowed skin, the mouth where someone pressed the letter "A" into the lips. Arms curling slightly along the rounded chest and stomach. Then coming to an abrupt stop as if a knife clipped the fingertips. One leg look looks slightly longer than the other. This is what happens when someone gathers dust from a New York City street on September 11, 2001, and stores it in a baggy. Afraid the customs officials would seize his baggie of dust, Xu Bing thought of his daughter. What if he cast the dust into a doll? Who would fear a doll? Once past customs, he placed the doll in a coffee blender and ground it back into dust. Then, in a sealed space, he blew the dust over a stencil with this Zen Buddhist question: "As there is nothing from the first /Where does the dust collect itself?" Now the 9/11 dust was transformed into Art. Not all agree. Critic Jerome du Bois offers this objection: "This is vampiric appropriation at its most visceral. On that horrible day whatever else he did Xu Bing took the time to *plan an artwork*. Can anyone know what's in Xu Bing's dust? Could there be pulverized remains of human beings . . . ?" And yet if this were dust from Normal Road during a drought, and it was blown over a stencil that read, "Is dust ever simply dust?" who would care? "It's just dust," we'd say. But Xu Bing's dust is sacred dust. Dust that inhibits, inhabits. In the eyes and lungs. Forces us to see everything as constructions of dust. Still, I would like to tell Xu Bing one thing. It's not the possession of 9/11 non violent living violent dust that disturbs. It's the doll.

The Infinity of the Finite, or Why My Name Comes Up Every Time a Sinkhole Is Found

I'm the historian of wart removal throughout the ages, hailstones as currency, strictures on eating crows, Band-Aids adhering to sidewalks, the use of Do-Wah-Diddy as curative, photographs of the letter X formed by trees, buttons made from glass eyes, welcome mats woven with human hair.

Historian of predictions of pencil lead snappage, translations of wind blab in chimneys, silence adhering to ball peen hammers, what stone does to paper when not monitored by scissors, the effect of hairspray on box-elder bugs, telephone poles used as sun dials, the sexual proclivities of the Galaxie 500 in southern Indiana.

I'm the historian of pink flamingo lawn ornament murders, purification methods for manhole covers, incidents of cell phone swallowings, time-lapse film footage of a school bus dissolved by the Mississippi, barbed wire fashioned by furloughed prisoners into sofas, accounts of aliens posing as a hot water heater.

Historian of vaseline usage per income level, stuttering frequency before earthquakes, studies of cheese grater apertures, artificial-limb-made music, signatures of atomic plant workers at five year intervals, field recordings of keening cats, remedies for eyebrow loss, the effect of Wheaties on traditional and nontraditional marriages.

Historian of Bo Diddley imitators, drills used for the human skull, regional thimble design, baggies containing termite eggs and a pocket watch, fedoras placed over brown spots on the lawn, the sound of a stomach trying to digest a marble, as recalled by elbow and maracas.

I'm the historian of the shape of children's hands in winter, dolls giving birth to doll furniture, mannequins found in smokestacks, toe erosion due to pumice stone usage, raccoon scat containing scraps of The Book of Evensong, ice cubes made with goat milk, the effect of moonlight on baldness in western Nebraska. Teeth carved with figures of rutting gods.

Leni Riefenstahl, The Final Installment

At 101, you can be reasonably preserved and yet someone will always ask for a refund. Helene Amalie Riefenstahl was born in an underwater community thirteen months before she was born on land. She once told Hitler at a dinner party that she felt horrible about the stain on her white silk blouse, and he reportedly took a pair of scissors and snipped out the offending birthmark. According to Charlie Chaplin, she slept with a swan, a castrated bell, and a pair of castanets. She studied shamanism, modern dance, dentistry, ballet, and Biblical carpentry. She loved to tell of how she made love to Robert Capa in Zurich on a trapeze, though he swore it happened on a speeding bicycle. Insert aphorism from *The Art of Forgetting* here. "The camera," she often said, "is not a razor blade or a truncheon, not a stick of butter or a star made of concrete, or a goat in an evening gown nor a mole on the moon." In Sudan, she wore leather pants and a white silk blouse with a wedding ring sewn into the right shoulder. "Film cannot make hairs grow on the chin," she explained, "but it can make the chin appear to be a planet where forests of hair reign." Immediately after her death, a board game was released, entitled *Triumph of The Ambidextrous*. "I had no idea," she claimed, "that one day Hitler would become a vegetarian repast." Wherever she had slept, seaweed would be found. When questioned about this, she replied, "Instead of complaining, make a salad." Hollywood filmmakers could not understand why she wanted to make a film where all the actors would be jellyfish. Asked how long it would take her to wash her hands, comb her hair, repair a broken chair, and boil a callus, she replied: "Six days, of course." One film critic writes of her films: "The backdrop of clouds is nothing more than what the earthworm sees when looking out at the world with its one good eye." And if a Mongolian earthworm is mistaken for a cloud? "I always admitted that, yes, in the beginning I was worm-fixated," she admitted, hair sprouting from her tongue. Insert *Items from Forged Menus* here. My mother, on the morning after Riefenstahl's death, left a message on my answering machine: "I told you— Germans make the best plumbing fixtures." Late in her life she wrote, "Every film I ever made was a comedy. Some will make your belly laugh and some your belly cry, but they are all comedies, every one."

In the Shop of the Tin Noses

I asked her what her hands did before the war: she held up a moth by its wings. The mask: galvanized copper the thickness of a visiting card. Sometimes I found him at the center of the headache. (*Click here* to watch injured World War I faces.) He said of the bullet that bloomed his skull: "A barrel of whitewash tipped over and it seemed that everything in the world turned white." With a flat drum hanging from my neck, I wandered: though my fingers recognized no one. She stared at his profile and drew: the melting of a bottle. The masks requested to be buried with their owners: seen now on raised granite plinth.

In the house of the drowsy flies, the woman I love lets me say: "The woman I love no longer finds me repulsive. As she has a right to do." A single mask requiring a mouth of close attention. Yet the drum never wilted. Imitate: the bluish tinge of shaven cheeks on a winter morning. When I rubbed the drum a certain way, it released a flesh-like keening. (Q. "Why are you pimp-walking in the hospital? A. "I'm not pimp-walking. I'm an amputee.") Remember: it's watching your face to see its face.

Then I saw her (the author of *National Velvet*) at the yard sale, sitting at the piano made from yard tools. The park bench painted blue: as a public warning. Eyebrows, eyelashes, mustaches she made from slivered tinfoil: not to be called a spectacle. I churned the _____ drum; the _____ drum churned me. At the Union of the Facially Blessed: always look straight into the faltering unseen.

Edward Teller, Father of Further and Farther

"Oppenheimer, Oppenheimer, isn't that the opera where everyone dies at the end?" he once asked Yogi Berra. At the University of Leipzig, he studied the physics of the leaping abilities of fleas. He toured the country briefly with his folk group Strategic Defense Initiative, which later became Brilliant Pebbles, a metal band. At the University of Chicago, he studied the physics of pan pizza. The first megaton H-Bomb was exploded in 1952, he joked, at the same moment that Marilyn Monroe was washing a pair of her stockings in a small sink. In 1919, his native Hungary forbade the use of woodburning box kites. Teller once made Ronald Reagan laugh so hard that fragments of sternum had to be removed from the President's colon. Then he would pull out his stopwatch. "I deeply regret the deaths and injuries that resulted from the atomic bombings," he wrote in his memoirs, "but my best explanation of why I do not regret working on weapons is a question: Who's your daddy?" For breakfast, an old tie, a few chess pieces, and some freshly squeezed garlic. "I am not the Father of the H-Bomb," Teller often stated. "I'm a conductor of atomic music as played on coconuts by a band of highly trained and highly gifted gorillas." Teller was born in Budapest, the city where one half never shaves and the other half spends all day and night shaving. With a piece of string, a forceps, and two drum sticks, he could make a three year old understand nuclear fruit flies. In secret interviews with the FBI, Teller revealed how to make boiled cabbage taste like black bean soup. Then he would pull out his stopwatch. His wife, Mici, could be seen erasing the zeroes in his equations and replacing them with tiny drawings of birds, carrots, and hailstorms. Some say this was a reminder for Teller to occasionally take a bath. At Lawrence Livermore Laboratory, he developed a severe allergic reaction to chalk dust, which he never publicly admitted. In 1941, on the day Teller and his wife became citizens, they bought a camera and made a short pornographic film, "Forty-Three Point Seven Seconds," now worth thousands of dollars. "A bomb is the glue of peace," Teller stated at a Colorado State University lecture. "The bigger the bomb, the stronger the glue." According to friends, he would steal the salami from Enrico Fermi's sandwiches, glue the two halves of bread together, and then pull out his stopwatch. No one in California currently going by the name of Edward Teller would say he was the father or son of the deceased Edward Teller. In Livermore, a small fire erupted in a private aquarium. "No symphony should ever run for more than one minute," Teller said, pulling out his stopwatch, thus bringing to a quick close every concert he attended, often to standing ovation.

Footnote to a Line by Fernando Pessoa

"I want to fly and fall from way up high!"[1]

---

1. In Charles Lindbergh's diary, composed after his transatlantic flight, he said that to stay awake in the *Spirit of St. Louis* he recited "lines from that great Portuguese poet what's-his-name." No doubt he was referring to Fernando Pessoa's "Salutation to Walt Whitman," by Alvaro de Campos. Perhaps the very line above. Some think, however, that this diary entry was meant as a challenge to those who later claimed that Lindbergh recited "99 Bottles of Beer on the Wall" during the flight. The implication being, of course, that the beer was German, a reference to Lindbergh's admiration of Nazi beer. Still other critics have argued that this entry was not written by Lindbergh, but inserted into Lindbergh's diary by Brendan Gill, a friend of Lindbergh's but also an admirer of Pessoa. If true, perhaps Gill meant it as a tribute to Walt Whitman, though friends of Gill insist that he thought Whitman's poetry "made Longfellow look good." Still others think Lindbergh's diary was ghostwritten by his wife, Anne Morrow, and she meant the entry to refer to Elizabeth Barrett Browning's *Sonnets from the Portuguese*. But a disgruntled copy editor, who detested sonnets, changed the line so it alluded to the free verse of Pessoa. The most intriguing account of the Lindbergh-Pessoa connection, however, comes from a member of Lindbergh's ground crew, a certain L. Hampton Moon. In an interview given in a Long Island tavern, Moon disclosed that an unknown person appeared at the airstrip shortly before Lindbergh's takeoff and paid Moon to place a book by Pessoa (though Moon

used the name "Pizarro," perhaps a combination of "Pessoa" and "Alvaro"?) in the cockpit of the *Spirit of St. Louis*. Moon, finding the request rather odd, didn't ask any questions as he wanted the money to acquire a rare boomerang for his collection. Years later, when Moon questioned Lindbergh about the incident, Lindbergh would only say, "Let the winds do as they will." A further complication of the story takes us to the Toledo Museum of Modern Art. There, in 1989, I came across a framed page, one having suffered intense saltwater and sun damage. From Pessoa's "Salutation to Walt Whitman," it was identical to page 98 of *Another Republic: 17 European & South American Writers*, edited by Charles Simic and Mark Strand (which includes four Pessoa poems translated by Edwin Honig). The anonymous "artist" who framed the page added a footnote to the line "I want to fly and fall from way up high!" That footnote read: "1. Imagine falling from 'way up high' and not remember member embering." When contacted recently, the museum staff could not find the Pessoa page, nor any record of it having ever appeared in the museum.

(Let Us All Reflect for a Moment Upon) Dick's Hatband

Given that some person or persons among us (who shall remain unnamed) have been called "weirder than Dick's hatband," be it resolved—

A) That in the earliest extant photograph of Dick, we see him in his yellow pajamas (with rubber-soled booties) appareled with his father's briefcase, pipe, and, of course, hat (though this is most likely not the infamous hat and hatband.)

B) That Dick's mother allegedly said to a hatmaker (who claims he never made hats but pickup truck covers): "That's weirder than Dick's bellybutton."

C) That the unmistakable hat/hatband was worn by Dick to a social gathering where he was tied to the hood of the car and driven at great speeds to see if he could be parted with hat and hatband, and while this theory does confer the status of victim on the person of Dick, he emerges as complicit in the above actions in that his wearing of the hat was obsessive, or at the very least excessive and provocative.

D) That both the aforementioned hat and hatband may be a willful and perhaps even skillful act of diverting our attention from the more pertinent matter —the size of Dick's head. Not that the size of Dick's head implies, of course, anything about Dick's sexual prowess or ability to slice a watermelon with a chainsaw while driving a Landrover through a herd of flamingoes.

E) That the unspecified hatband was not a hatband at all but a euphemism for a socially unapproved of act or series of acts that Dick performed in the privacy of his hat. (There is one incident involving an anonymous female on a Greyhound bus who states that Dick, seated next to her on the bus, opened his fly and displayed, according to this source, "a tiny fedora on his dong." The charge must be qualified, however, by the fact the accuser later admitted to having eaten nothing but black licorice for the previous 72 hours.)

F) That having never experienced the molecular structure commonly known as Dick, all we can say about Dick and his vexatious hatband can be what Dick was once overheard saying to himself (and his hat and hatband):

> *Lordy Lordy*
> *Lordy Lordy*
> *Lordy Lordy Lord.*

I Think I Hear the President Commuting the Silence of

a Meandering Carnivorous Sentence

Number Theory

"You mean you don't know how old your own father is?" says my mother. "Your father's two hundred and sixty-eight years old. He's been that way for twenty-four years." I hold the phone and stare out the back window. Each particle of rain bears the story of every other particle of rain. If you combined all of those raindrops into the shape of a dog, would the dog when it died begin to rain? "Are you still there?" my mother asks. "But if he's two-hundred and sixty-eight," I wonder, "how can you still be sixteen?"

Parable of the Indeterminate Cave

I'm living in a sealed cave with Madonna. At least she tells me her name is Madonna, but I'm not so sure. She never wants to have sex, though I've tried many times to subtly suggest it. I'll tell her that an oak chair was left out in the rain, and she'll say that wet wooden chairs make her depressed. I'll say that a glazed doughnut is rolling down a hill, and she'll say that doughnuts make her feel fat. I'll say that a child is sleeping with his head on the stretched skin of a drum, and she'll tell me that drum skins make her perspire. There is one thing Madonna does like, though. She likes it when I read to her. Sometimes I read her knuckles to her, though I usually read her toes. I'll read until I start to get bored, and then I'll change a word in the story. I'll say, "Father stroked his seersucker mustache," and she'll yell at me. "That's not right," she'll say. "Father stroked his cerise mustache!"

I Was John and Cindy McCain's Indentured Servant

I prefer a master severe, yet soft; soft, yet severe. Ancient land reptiles roamed the sea of Kansas reading Darwin's *The Origin of Something We Better Not Talk About*. I pour my mistress a cup of coffee, and she pours the contents into the milk carton, shakes it, and then waits for me to serve her. The very mention of the word "science" makes me want to study your bodily fluids. My mistress prefers a servant meek, yet mute; mute, yet meek. The very mention of the word "erotic" makes me want to rub my epidermis against a tree that has yet to be planted or pulped. Limbs initially designed for holding *The Wall Street Journal* can evolve back into an axe-like appendage. In my master's private bathroom, I read his leather-bound copy of Dostoevsky's *The Idiot*, tearing out the gilt-edged pages for toilet paper. The very mention of the word "servant" makes me want to adopt Arthur "Killer" Kane as my personal savior. Should my mistress ask, I prefer my sexual partner servile, yet surly; surly, yet servile.

Parable of the Unclean Litter

When the intruder entered, I was up on the third floor landing, leaning over the low wooden railing, litter box in one hand and a long-handled shovel in the other. A shovel big enough to dig up a small fruit tree. How the shovel got on the third floor, I still don't know, but when the cat litter stuck to the bottom of the box, I couldn't find the plastic rake, so I wandered around until I found the shovel. The blade was way too big, of course, to get the piss-stuck-litter out of the corner, so I had to hang the box over the railing, angle the blade just so, and then I could scrape loose the damn litter, finally, out of the corner. That's when I heard him. A door slammed somewhere below, the basement door or the door from the garage, and I yelled down to whomever had the nerve to break into our house while I was cleaning the cat box: Hey! I saw the top of his head down there three flights below in the main landing, and that's when it happened.

Into my brain came the news from afar: The wooden handle was sliding through my fingers. Like the time I was playing flag football and my fingertips stroked the plastic flag dangling just out of reach from the belt around John Roberts's waist. To this day I think he had his flag wrapped around the belt so it wouldn't come loose. That shovel went down and down and down as if it wanted nothing more in the world than to be buried into my father's head. My father, God bless him, looked up at the spade coming down at him like the one story of his life he couldn't deny, the only one that made sense, not like the time he got the crabs and gave them to my mother and tried to tell her he got them from a gas station toilet seat. Maybe he was telling the truth. You can believe almost anything hanging over the third floor railing with a litter box in your hand.

Sam Cooke Teaches Richard Nixon the Twist

Little known American history: Nixon, while wrenching his body back and forth, asked Cooke, "Sam, besides twistin' the night away, what is it the American Negro really wants?" In 1962, when a rope crossed the concert hall dividing blacks and whites. In 1962, when some women stopped wearing chastity belts. Is it true, Sam, you added the "e" to the end of your name in order to keep dust from collecting in the sharp corners of the "k"? "When Nixon did the twist," Cooke told a friend, "that brother looked like he was trying to put out a fire on the back of a live chicken." True or False: "A Change Is Gonna Come" was released as the B-side of "Shake," for a shake must always precede a change. In 1962, when the moon still obeyed the laws of refrigerated cheese. In 1962, when nine out of ten Americans believed you could get cancer from oral sex. Is it true, Sam, you added the "e" because you were afraid of choking on the "k"? Three bullets, the feet grind back and forth. Three bullets, with very little vertical motion. Three bullets, the arms more or less stationary. After Cooke's death, Nixon, with one leg lifted off the floor for styling, stated, "Well, his songs weren't very consequential, but that man sure knew how to sweat up a crowd." Some parents, arms held out from the body, called the dance obscene due to the "pelvic motions." Final bonus point—True or False: Cooke cooed to the woman who shot him, "Lady, a change is gonna come."

Confessions of a Ladder Rider

I'm riding my ladder down the street, one of those fast, lightweight folding ladders, standing on it a few steps from the bottom, wearing my white riding helmet. She's crossing the street, her blouse aswirl with STOP and YIELD and RAILROAD CROSSING signs. When she sees me coming at her, she freezes. In order to avoid hitting her, I swerve to the left, assuming she'll continue across the street. But she doesn't. The ladder catches her with the center of the wooden X right on her chin, and she flops down on her back like a sack of wilted celery. I let out, just for a second, a nervous laugh. I knew she wasn't hurt, and the sight of her going down like that tickled me, the way silent film turns fall into farce. I immediately try to apologize, but my muffled giggling only makes things worse. There had been a rash of hit-and-run ladder riders knocking down pedestrians, and she must have thought I was one of them. I would have felt the same way, if I were her. I rip off my helmet; she faints. Did she see the mark of the folding ladder on my forehead? Had she eaten celery for lunch? Why wasn't she wearing her pedestrian body armor? O, Buster Keaton, why did you ever have to invent the motorized ladder? I fasten my helmet strap, climb back aboard my vehicle, and fade into the flow of traffic, just another outlaw ladder rider.

Sometimes My Skin Flies Off in Tiny Particles and Then Some Time Later Flies Back And Acts As If It Never Left, But That Has Nothing To Do With What I'm About To Tell You

A stationary shadow beneath a white van in the parking lot by the little one-room school house. It breaks loose from the van and the ground and starts humping away at the underside of the van. Only it isn't a shadow but a guy in suit and tie, his hips pumping up and down like they're trying to suck the oil pan dry. I zoom in closer, maybe too close. I begin to slide out of my body and into the camera, out through the lens, and into the guy humping the van.

Now I don't know how this can happen, but I think it probably happens a lot, only people are afraid to tell you about it. I think it happened to Ronald Reagan, and maybe to Mother Teresa, and a few times to Robert Frost, but I'm not sure. All I know is I'm underneath this van, humping away, and I start to feel sick, chunks of concrete cities whirling around in my stomach. I slide out from under the van, look up at the sun, and proceed down the path that follows the curve of the river.

As it is written in *The Book of Rapture* (17:2): "The river never floweth unto the path, and the path never floweth unto the river, and the river keepeth thanking me for not humping it." The sun, white eye at its center, studies my every move.

All the Ape-Gone Songs

"Where are all the ape-gone songs?" wondered the man without thumbs. "Look at your hands. You're obviously short a couple thumbs," said the spokesperson for The Office of Song Protection. "If I had even one song, why I could have lift, and loft, and Weltanschauung. And maybe even avian sex," noted the thumbless man. "Perhaps there's a global thumb shortage," reported the Song Protectionist. "Did someone just warble?" sang the man without two songs. "I swear I heard a sound a bird might make if it had thumbs where it once had wings."

I Think I Hear the Last Transmission in a World

of Lastlessness

The Figure in the Flux

"There's something missing, some little piece of the flux," said the figure in the flux. "Maybe a tiny piece of you is what's missing," said the flux. "Or maybe the missing piece is thinking right now that I'm missing," said the figure. "Or maybe you're missing and yet not missing, just like me," said the flux, who was being sucked, even as it spoke, back into the flux.

Parable of the Hair Chair

"What can you do with a chair made of hair?" I said. And it said, "Due to its lightness, it would be ideal for icicle removal." "OK," I said, taking the hint, and I ran out of the house with the chair over my head. I swung the chair at the icicles hanging from the roof, but the chair was too delicate. The icicles mocked the chair, calling it folliclely challenged. I swung the chair harder, but all I succeeded in doing was causing the hair to melt into a sticky black substance that smelled like burnt hair. In another version of this story, the chair strikes the icicle in such a way as to give off a music suitable for attracting fish to an ice fishing hole. But not in this version. "What can you do with a chair made of hair?" I said to the chair. "Take it to a fire alarm box, place it directly under the alarm, and leave a folded newspaper on the seat," it said. So I said, "In another version, icicles appear along the rim of the seat." And it said, "Yes, but not in this version."

You Too Can Apologize to the Moon

I dial 0-000-000-0000 and ask to speak with the moon.

"Who?" a young voice asks.

Perhaps this is a test, a doubling and tripling of resistance in order to produce an irresistible, iridescent plea.

"I'd like to speak to The Unlimited Night Sky Illumination System, The Light So Luscious It Must Be Stolen, The Shape That's Always Changing Shape, you know, the Moon," I say, adding, "to, um, apologize."

"And what would you wish to apologize for?" the voice replies, as if posing a routine question.

"Is this conversation being recorded?" I wonder aloud. "I mean, this is kind of personal, don't you think?"

"I'll take a message that you called, intending to apologize for personal, unspecified reasons. Thank you for your concern," she adds, and hangs up.

"I wish to apologize for . . . ," I begin, peering through the blinds at a jagged rip in the night sky.

Don't Blame the Chalk; I'd Rather Be Servicing Mr. & Mrs. Caulk

Mr. & Mrs. Caulk

take a short walk, come home, and seal their lips with white thread. The weatherperson feels a cocoon coming. "I feel so calm in cotton," says someone you and I don't (yet) know. I've lost my globe, the black and tan one I've never owned. Gravity washes its transparent hands. Mrs. Caulk, dropping the handwrought ceramic bowl on her foot, yowls, denaturing her and Mr. Caulk's oligarchic cat.

Mr. & Mrs. Caulk

make a frightful dog with a piece of chalk. I would not argue while sipping slippery bark tea. You can turn on some TVs while you're not even home. Pleasure wears socks that sag below the ankles. The dog bites Mrs. Caulk and she spites Mr. Caulk. You can see why I carry a small monkey with a spare key. Guido tows a howitzer made of balsa wood. The dog chews on Bolivia and the Florida Keys.

Mr. Caulk

goes about the house looking for Mrs. Caulk. A jar of black olives can let you see in the dark. The room whirls around so fast it can't recall kiss or slap. "This must be the year of the sick sofa," says Mrs. Caulk. Entropy makes me horny. I let Mrs. Caulk know I'm wondering what's moldering below her cleanly feet, and she flips on the garbage disposal so she can privately weep.

Mrs. Caulk

takes off her top on the back porch as it's too hot and no one's around. I feel sorry for Mr. Caulk, in the basement with a tuning fork. The table looks clean and strong, but can it hold a trombone? I lift a sandwich above my head to check for leaks. Eros hints an egg sandwich turns her on. A pimple poses unavoidable questions. Mr. Caulk grows into his hat, which scares Mrs. Caulk, which causes her toes to tingle.

Mr. & Mrs. Caulk

fall asleep on the front lawn. No one measures how little they grow, how long they shrink. I lithograph Mr. Caulk's unposed nose; it can't hurt. A house made of dirt isn't necessarily dirty. Molina thinks songs mutate into pie, shoe, bra. I shave Mrs. Caulks' legs while she's still asleep; I'm of age. That speck of blood behind the door. It makes me wonder if I'll have to come back here and do this all once more.

Asleep Inside a Bird

"Maybe it'll be easier to see the picture of Dan if we stand with our backs to him," my father suggests. Each time I had tried to look at it, the too high framed picture of my brother, it made my eyes burn,

If you fall

though there was no source of light, direct or indirect, from the glass in the frame. I had tried looking off to the side and then, after my eyes adapted, I'd stare, for a second of a second, directly

If you fall asleep

at the picture. An eclipse of the sun. At that moment, I wanted to say something harsh, something hurtful because I thought my father was telling me to give up on my brother, yet knowing how badly his heart was

If you fall asleep inside

damaged from his pneumonia, I didn't say anything. To make him feel as if he hasn't suggested anything improper, I nod, join him, side by side with our backs to the picture. After a while I can see my brother

If you fall asleep inside a bird

behind us, flashing his "What fools these mortals be" smile. But when I turn my head quickly to catch him, nothing but salted light. "You're right," I say to my father, "But how did you know this would work?"

If you fall asleep inside a bird, you'll wake

"Oh, it's nothing," he shrugs. "An old paratrooper trick. Look away from the object you want to spot." "See, see," I hear my brother start in. "Shut up," I tell him, "and copy this down on your palm."

If you fall asleep inside a bird, you'll wake up miles away from where you were.

Sustain

My shirt, my steep blue shirt, is sleeping. My mouth is sleeping. In my ankle an on-and-off twinge, on-and-off blood song. Aunt Betty really was my aunt and really was named Betty, though she lives now in my liver, fingernails, hair, respiration. She can still hear her daughter and husband argue as only Louise and Frank can: How many steps do you step to board the city bus when the city bus door opens at the concrete corner of Avenue N? Would Aunt Betty still be alive today if she had read *The Book of Angelic Lungs and Orderly Aorta*? Above my aorta there's an attic where spiders read the only book they read, *Spin, My Spinerette*. Each day they weave another book inside the book. In which moths confess they are not moths, but mouths. I am a mouth, but I keep it safely inside my chest, inside my steep blue shirt. I like long lines better than short lines because of the way they sustain. I once stood in a line to kiss a girl named Vickie, for which privilege I paid a quarter. Which is why Walt Whitman hugged saplings late in his elder years. "Sustain, that's how I play the piano," says Tori Amos, who is part Cherokee and part sustain and part Tori Amos. If you listen to the blood, every sound is song, every song the same sound. Saliva elevates the mouth, if you ask saliva. My shirt is awake, if you ask my shirt. My mouth is awake, or nearly so. The tongue somewhere in between. Bruno Ganz must be awake, in his steep blue shirt, which is also awake, reading *The Book of Bruno Schultz*, though he thinks it is *The Book of Nearly So*, which thinks of itself as an act of respiration. Making a salad, waking a carrot with a clutch of garlic. The spiders and moths, they wake one through the other. For the sake of something other, you and I sustain.

Crown

For my untold accomplishments over the untold years, they presented me with a crown, a crown of hair. It rested so lightly upon my hands it was as if it were made of air. Ah, and such finely wrought straw it was. Then, spotting a flaw, I froze. Was this an insult? A mistake? A joke? The hair my crown was woven with was none other than my own. Then again, whose hair was more fitting for a crown, and not just any crown but one crafted for this singular skull? The crowd waited, the lights shone, the crown glowed. I lifted it up and let the crown down upon my head. Rising to their feet, the crowd gasped for air.

Photo: Jana Brubaker

John Bradley is the author of *Love-In-Idleness: The Poetry of Roberto Zingarello* (Word Works), *Terrestrial Music* (Curbstone), and *War on Words* (BlazeVOX). He edited *Atomic Ghost: Poets Respond to the Nuclear Age* (Coffee House Press), *Learning to Glow: A Nuclear Reader* (University of Arizona Press), and *Eating the Pure Light: Homage to Thomas McGrath* (Backwaters Press). He teaches at Northern Illinois University and lives in DeKalb, Illinois, with his wife, Jana, and their cats, Kiki and Zuzu.